Back to the Wild

Back to the Wild

DOROTHY HINSHAW PATENT
Photos by WILLIAM MUÑOZ

A Gulliver Green Book

Harcourt Brace & Company

San Diego   New York   London

Library of Congress Cataloging-in-Publication Data
Patent, Dorothy Hinshaw
Back to the Wild/by Dorothy Hinshaw Patent;
photographs by William Muñoz.
p. cm.
"Gulliver Green."
Summary: Describes efforts to save endangered animals from extinction by breeding them
in captivity, teaching them survival skills, and then releasing them into the wild.
ISBN 0-15-200280-4
1. Wildlife reintroduction—Juvenile literature. 2. Endangered species—Juvenile literature.
3. Captive wild animals—Breeding—Juvenile literature. [1. Wildlife reintroduction.
2. Endangered species—Breeding. 3. Captive wild animals—Breeding.] I. Muñoz, William, ill. II. Title.
QL83.4.P38 1997
639.9'79—dc20 95-43254

C E F G D B

Printed in Singapore

Gulliver Green® books focus on various aspects of ecology and the environment,
and a portion of the proceeds from the sale of these books is donated to
protect, preserve, and restore native forests.

The photographs in this book were taken with Pentax MX cameras, using
a variety of lenses, from 28mm to 500mm, and Fujichrome 100 slide film.
The display type was set in Cerigo.
The text type was set in Meridien.
Color separations by United Graphic, Singapore
Printed and bound by Tien Wah Press, Singapore
This book was printed on totally chlorine-free Nymolla Matte Art paper.
Production supervision by Stanley Redfern
Designed by Lydia D'moch

Acknowledgments

The author and the photographer wish to thank Alligator River National Wildlife Refuge, Cape
Romain National Wildlife Refuge, Cincinnati Zoo and Botanical Garden, Duke University Primate
Center, Fossil Rim Wildlife Center, Henry Doorly Zoo, the IUCN's Species Survival Commission,
Knoxville Zoological Gardens, Lincoln Park Zoo, Lowry Park Zoo, Minnesota Zoological Garden,
Montana Department of Fish, Wildlife, and Parks, National Bison Range Refuge, Point Defiance
Zoo and Aquarium, Rio Grande Zoological Park, and the U.S. Fish and Wildlife Service for their
cooperation with this book. We also want to thank Ben Beck, Sue Behrns, Kenneth Glander,
David Haring, V. Gary Henry, Randy Matchett, Lex Salisbury, Roland Smith,
Ron Stoneberg, Tom Thorne, and Will Waddell.

For all those involved in saving species, especially Sue.
Thank you.

—D. P. and W. M.

CONTENTS

Introduction

viii

Vanishing Wilderness

2

Return of the Red Wolf

12

The Black-Footed Ferret

28

The Golden Lion Tamarin

40

Leaping Lemurs

50

Hope and Disappointment

60

INTRODUCTION

Across the face of planet Earth, natural habitats are being destroyed by humans at a rate never before experienced. As more and more people are born, they need places to live and to grow food. In wealthy countries like the United States, land is cleared for new vacation homes, condominiums, and shopping malls. And in forests around the Earth, trees are felled for lumber and paper, destroying the homes of countless plant and animal species.

Many life-forms are disappearing completely because of these activities. But for some species, there is hope. Plants and animals can be bred in captivity in the safety of an environment free of natural and human-made dangers until their numbers have increased. Then, with careful planning and plenty of money, they can be returned to the wild once there are safe places for them to live. This process of captive breeding for reintroduction into the wild is a relatively new and expanding area of scientific effort that involves the cooperation of scientists, zoos, parks and preserves, and governments around the world.

This book presents some of the highlights in just one area of this new science—the breeding and reintroduction of large mammals such as American red wolves and lemurs from Madagascar. In the process, the problems and pitfalls of captive breeding programs are shown, along with the successes. It is far preferable never to reduce living things to endangered status in the first place. But when it happens, we are finding out how to save at least some species from the oblivion of extinction.

Back to the Wild

CHAPTER 1

Vanishing
Wilderness

THE TERMS *ENDANGERED SPECIES* AND *EXTINCTION* are currently subjects of everyday conversation. It wasn't always like that. When I was a child, vast wild places inhabited by mysterious creatures existed on every continent. I spent hours poring over books recounting the adventures of brave explorers who risked their lives to collect specimens of exotic wildlife for zoos. Extinction was something that had happened long ago to the dinosaurs, or more recently, to the dodo bird and the passenger pigeon. It wasn't happening anymore—at least that is what people seemed to think.

As I grew up, the ever increasing human population of our planet took over most wild places, and the process continues today. We struggle to keep some wildlands in the United States, where almost all of the country is ruled by humans rather than nature. To the south, around the equator, tropical rain forests,

Barred cages like this one used to be
the accepted way of exhibiting animals in zoos.

which are home to the greatest variety of both plant and animal species, are disappearing before the ax and fire at the alarming rate of fifty acres an hour. Without homes, wild things cannot survive.

Loss of their homes, or habitat, is not the only problem facing wildlife. In many parts of the world, people have been hunting some species almost to extinction. These animals are valued for their meat, for their beautiful fur coats, or for magical properties their body parts are believed to possess.

When I was young, I often visited the zoo, but I hated it as much as I loved it. Back then, zoos were places designed for people, not for the animals. Their goal was to exhibit the variety of animal life on earth in a way that made it easy for

The cheetah is endangered because it is hunted for its beautiful coat. The coat of the rare king cheetah, pictured here, is especially prized.

people to view it. Seeing the beautiful and strange animals was wonderful. But watching how they suffered by living in small concrete cages was painful. I hated watching the African hunting dogs pace back and forth, back and forth, across the front of their cage. I almost cried when I saw a huge male gorilla sitting on the cold floor of his sterile cage, staring straight ahead at nothing.

Many zoos in the Western world are now completely different from what I used to experience. They are no longer first and foremost exhibitions but are becoming homes for wild creatures. These zoo homes meet at least some of the animals' needs beyond food and protection from disease. Zoos now consider themselves modern arks, new versions of Noah's fabulous boat that was supposed to have carried a pair of every kind of animal during the great flood. The zoo ark strives to preserve wild creatures and to give them an opportunity to reproduce their kind.

The goal of a number of zoo programs goes beyond breeding simply to maintain a captive population. Rare animals are bred in captivity specifically for release into the wild. These programs are designed to help right a wrong, and to try to restore some of the natural balance lost as our species has taken over the planet.

The idea of breeding animals that will be put back into the wild is not a new one. During the settling of the American West, the bison that once roamed the plains by the millions were reduced to only a few hundred animals, almost all in captivity. Fortunately, bison breed well. In 1907, fifteen were released on a reserve in Oklahoma, followed by more onto

*Animals, like this serval, have room
to run and explore in today's zoos.*

the National Bison Range in Montana. Today, over 100,000 bison live in the wild in a number of American parks and preserves.

While the American bison was being restored in the wild, its European cousin was disappearing. The European bison, also called the wisent, became extinct in the wild in 1925. From then until the 1950s, it survived only in zoos and private preserves. At that time, some animals were released into the Bialowieza Forest in Poland. The wisent thrived and now numbers almost three thousand.

Becoming wild again isn't always so easy. Because animals differ in how they obtain the knowledge necessary for survival, some adapt easily to the independence they experience after release, while the shift is more difficult for others. Learning how to survive in the wild is relatively simple for large grazing animals like bison. Their food is easy to obtain, and their former natural enemies, such as wolves, are absent from their wild homes. Bison are born with most of the tools they need for survival. Calves stand within minutes of birth and can run when only three hours old. They begin nibbling grass within a few days of being born and are independent of their mothers by the time they are a year old. Their enormous size alone is good protection against predators that might attack. They need little guidance from their elders.

Adapting to the wild is much more difficult for animals that need to learn from others of their kind how to feed and how to protect themselves. Animals such as orangutans have a completely different lifestyle from the bison. These intelligent

Though bison calves need to be fed and protected from danger by their mothers, they are born with the basic skills they need for survival.

apes are born helpless and are cared for by their mothers for many years. The mothers teach them to find food and how to protect themselves in their complex forest habitat. Orangutans that grow up in zoos have no knowledge of where to find food and what is safe to eat. They do not know how to protect themselves, as their lives in captivity are devoid of danger. Because they are used to humans and associate people with food, if released into the wild they are likely to end up near villages where they are at risk of being killed or captured. Captive orangutans also lack the physical strength gained in the wild from strenuous daily activities. Hundreds of orangutans rescued from the pet

Right: Orangutans learn how to survive in the wild from their mothers.

trade have been released in the forests of Sumatra and Borneo, and no one knows how many, if any, learned to survive.

Predators—animals that catch and kill other animals for food—may also have problems adapting to a wild life. Like captive orangutans, they won't have developed physical strength, and hunting requires a strong body with a great deal of stamina. They haven't learned how to stalk, chase, and kill healthy wild prey because their food is provided for them and is dead when they get it.

As more and more endangered animals end up in zoos, scientists and zookeepers have been learning both how to get them to breed and how to help them develop the survival skills needed for return to the wild, if that is their destiny.

These goals can clash with one another. When only a few individuals of a species survive, each individual is precious.

The animals are raised and tended carefully. Any risk to their survival is avoided, and efforts are focused on getting them to reproduce as rapidly as possible. The needs of animals slated for release into the wild are quite different. They must be able to survive hardship—they will face hunger, predators, disease, and bad weather. The methods used to teach the animals how to deal with these problems bring some necessary risks into their lives, but they prepare them for freedom.

In addition to the mammals we will learn about in this book, several kinds of birds have already been successfully returned to their wild homes. With each reintroduction, scientists learn more about the kinds of problems the animals will face, which gives them the information they need to make the animals' transition from captivity to the wild easier the next time.

The countries of the world have their own rules for listing living things as endangered. But governments and zoos around the world do cooperate through the International Union for the Conservation of Nature and Natural Resources (IUCN). Both governmental and nongovernmental agencies belong to this organization, which was founded in 1948 through the United Nations. Efforts to save endangered species are coordinated with the help of the IUCN, which performs many important functions, including compiling the *Red Data Book,* an official listing of endangered species around the world. The American Zoo Association, in cooperation with the IUCN, has the responsibility of preparing a document called the Species Survival Plan (SSP) for each endangered species. So far, only a small number of endangered animals have an SSP. The plan maps out the goals for

that species. How many individuals of the species still live in the wild? How many in zoos? How should the captive animals be bred? Should captive-bred animals be released into the wild? If so, when, where, and how?

Once a species is endangered, helping it recover is a very expensive and time-consuming process, and success is not guaranteed. More reintroductions have failed than have succeeded. But when a reintroduction effort does succeed, it helps restore balance to a natural system that cannot function well without all the necessary parts. Each species in a particular environment interacts with the other species that live there. The disappearance of one species affects all the others that live in that environment. It is comforting to know that not all the mistakes we make are forever. We can correct some of them.

Return of the Red Wolf

I COULDN'T BELIEVE MY LUCK—I was actually going to be able to look in on a mother red wolf and her pups. Along with Roland Smith, at that time red wolf species coordinator, I carefully got down on my hands and knees in front of the concrete structure that was the mother wolf's den. Roland swung the flashlight around and there she was, lying on her side, her pups curled up along her belly. She reached down with her muzzle and gently licked one of the wriggly, furry bundles. She was an unusual red wolf, not leery of people. Because her mother had died when she was born, she had been raised by Sue Behrns, the devoted manager of the red wolf breeding facility. Roland reached in and carefully removed two reluctant pups. They opened their tiny mouths and growled, and they bared their sharp little milk teeth and did their best to bite. They were fierce little beasts, good candidates for eventual life in the wild.

A red wolf

When Europeans first came to North America, two kinds of wolves lived here. The familiar gray wolf, also called the timber wolf, roamed over most of the continent, from the East Coast through the forests, plains, and mountains all the way to the West, and from the wilds of northern Canada and Alaska southward into Mexico. But in a small region of the humid South, a different wolf made its home. With its short-hair coat, long legs, bigger ears, and smaller size, the red wolf was adapted to life in the thick vegetation of the hot, humid southland.

Both kinds of wolves had trouble sharing the land with people. Wolves sometimes killed the livestock people raised for food, so, in turn, humans killed wolves. As human settlement took over the Southeast, the red wolf was pushed deeper and deeper into swamps that were unfit for farming. By the 1960s, the wolves were almost gone. Only small numbers survived in parts of southern Louisiana and Texas. The few remaining animals often had trouble finding mates and were

A gray wolf

breeding with their close relatives, coyotes. It looked like the end for the red wolf.

In 1973, the U.S. Congress passed the Endangered Species Act, for the first time giving the government the power to take steps to save plants and animals faced with extinction. The red wolf *(Canis rufus),* already officially listed as endangered, was one of the first animals to be included as endangered under this law. When a species is listed as endangered, a recovery plan is supposed to be written describing the steps to be taken to try to save it from extinction.

The Red Wolf Recovery Plan called for trapping red wolves in the wild and determining which individuals were pure red wolves and which were coyote hybrids. The pure red wolves would then be bred in captivity with an eye to releasing them later into the wild. The plan was risky—no one had ever bred a predator in captivity for a number of generations and then released it to fend for itself. But for the red wolf, there was really no choice. The few remaining animals were living in a poor habitat where they could barely survive. They were plagued by parasites like hookworms and heartworms, and their skin was infested with the tiny mites that cause sarcoptic mange, a disorder that causes terrible itching and can lead to death.

The capture operation occupied biologists from 1974 to 1978. During that time, they trapped a total of four hundred coyotes, red wolves, and hybrids. Each animal was weighed and measured, and its skull was X-rayed. The coyotes and hybrids were treated for their diseases and then released. If a particular animal appeared to be a pure red wolf, it was bred

to see if its offspring were pure. After the forty-three animals in this group were tested, only seventeen were found to be pure. Three did not successfully breed, so just fourteen animals became founders of the current population. By 1980, it became clear that no more red wolves remained in the wild.

The U.S. Fish and Wildlife Service was put in charge of the few remaining wolves. It asked zoos to help breed the animals in captivity, but only the Point Defiance Zoo in Tacoma, Washington, was willing to cooperate. None of the zoos in the wolf's southland home would take on the job. There was one advantage to sending the wolves to Washington, however—heartworm was absent from the state, so the wolves would be free of that disease.

When an endangered species is bred in captivity, matings must be carefully arranged or animals could breed with close relatives, which can bring out genetic diseases. Individuals with a unique genetic heritage might become underrepresented in later generations, further reducing the already sparse genetic diversity of the species. For these reasons, a studbook is kept for each endangered species that is bred in captivity. The history and pedigree of each animal is listed in the studbook: whether it was captured in the wild or bred in captivity, who its parents were, when it was born, and where it lives now. Using this information, decisions are made about which animals to mate to maintain as much genetic diversity as possible.

Fortunately, the wolves bred easily in captivity, and by the late 1970s, the zoo already had more wolves than it could house—sixty-three, to be exact. A nearby mink rancher volunteered to help out and leased five acres of his land to the project for a symbolic fee of a dollar a year.

In 1983, other zoos were asked to join in the red wolf recovery effort. If the sixty-three red wolves could be separated and bred in a number of locations, a disease outbreak wouldn't wipe out the species scientists had worked so hard to save. Many zoos responded this time and built breeding pens. Before long the red wolf population doubled, and scientists felt there were enough animals to chance releasing some into the wild. The problem was deciding how and where to carry out releases.

When the U.S. Fish and Wildlife Service began to look for a place to reintroduce red wolves, it ran into the old prejudices people had against these predators. People had done their best to get rid of wolves; why should they welcome them back again? Farmers were afraid the wolves would kill their livestock, and hunters feared deer populations would decline. Landowners didn't want use of their land restricted because an endangered species lived there. Scientists felt that if the wolves were placed where coyotes lived, they would need to remove the coyotes to keep them from breeding with the wolves, but since coyotes are so common in most of the country and are usually not welcomed by ranchers and farmers, captured coyotes would have to be killed. Animal rights activists objected strongly.

Hope of a solution came in 1984 when 118,000 acres of land in eastern North Carolina was donated to the government and became the Alligator River National Wildlife Refuge. The region was prime red wolf habitat with potential prey animals such as raccoons, deer, and rabbits. It was also free of coyotes. The land was a peninsula surrounded on three sides by water, which would help keep the animals contained on public lands. It seemed like a perfect place for the wolves.

The original Endangered Species Act prohibited people from moving or killing individuals of an endangered species, even if they were causing trouble for humans. But in 1982, the act was amended to allow for an "experimental population" to be established. Since the released animals were designated to be surplus—individuals not needed for breeding in captivity—they could be moved around or even killed if they began attacking livestock or leaving the refuge and living on private land where they were not welcome. Hunters and trappers could also continue to use the refuge without restrictions

Farmlands border dense vegetation near the Alligator River National Wildlife Refuge.

aimed at protecting red wolves, which would have been difficult before the amendment.

Luckily for the red wolf, most of the few people living near the public land were in favor of the reintroduction plan, and approval was swift. They realized that the wolves would bring tourist dollars to their region, and the wolf biologists were able to gain residents' trust by ensuring that human interests as well as those of the wolves would be taken into account after the animals were released.

Now came the hard part. How should the wolves be reintroduced into the wild? Which wolves should be used? What could be done to help the animals develop the skills they would need to survive on their own? And what was the best way to keep track of them once they were free? The scientists working on the project thought long and hard about these issues. The fate of the individual animals they had helped bring into the world was their responsibility, and the

Before being released into the wild, red wolves are kept in pens at the release site so that they become accustomed to staying in that area.

success or failure of the species in the wild depended on them as much as on the wolves themselves.

Four pairs of wolves were picked for the first releases, all with plenty of close relatives in the breeding program. That way, if they didn't survive in the wild, their genetic contribution to the species wouldn't be lost. Each pair had already successfully produced litters of pups, but the recovery of the wild red wolf depended on the ability of the animals to reproduce in the new environment.

How to release the wolves? Only once had a release attempt been made, on an island off the North Carolina coast. At that time, a pair of wild Texas red wolves had been put in a pen for five weeks, then released. The female wolf left the island and swam to the mainland, where recapturing her wasn't easy. She and her mate were again penned, this time for six months. When they were released a second time, they stayed on the island.

This experience showed that the wolves needed to become used to their new home before being released. Four sites on the refuge were chosen and chain-link pens for the wolves were built. A caretaker lived near each site to watch the wolves and keep people away.

Keeping the wolves wary of humans was important to their eventual success in the wild, but they also needed to hunt and kill their own food. For the first two months in the pens, the wolves were fed the same dry dog food they had always eaten. Then, carcasses of deer, raccoon, opossum, squirrel, rabbit, and nutria—all wild foods they would find on the refuge—were given to them. The animals had been killed by cars or donated by hunters who wanted to help the wolves.

To check on their hunting skills, biologists released a few live animals into the pens. Luckily, the wolves were easily able to kill their prey, which was a great relief. Bit by bit, the wolves were adjusted to an irregular feeding schedule. Wild predators eat when food is available. They may gorge themselves on a deer carcass one day, then have to wait a week before another successful hunt. The penned wolves were fed every other day, then every four days, to get them used to the cycle of gorging and feeling hungry.

When the time for release neared, each wolf was fitted with a special collar that weighed about a pound and contained a battery and a radio transmitter that produced a beep on a radio receiver. Each collar beeped at a different radio frequency so biologists could easily track the location of each wolf by using a handheld antenna or one attached to the wing of an airplane.

In the fall of 1987, the captive pairs were released one by one. The moment of freedom was not dramatic. After a final health check and weigh-in, the wolves were fed, but the door to the pen was left open when the people left. The wolves didn't rush for the open door with excitement; they were used to the pen, which had become home. But bit by bit, the wolves explored the area near their pens and eventually abandoned them. Some pairs stayed together but others split up, and the biologists kept busy trying to keep track of them.

No one expected all the animals to survive. They were not used to life in the wild and to taking care of themselves. Roads

The adults in this red wolf family already wear the radio collars that enable scientists to track the wolves after release.

With a soft release, the door to the wolves' pen is simply left open. They can leave to explore and still return to the familiarity of the pen if they want to.

Signs along highways
warn motorists to watch
out for red wolves.

Roads are
convenient pathways
for wolves, just as they
are for people.

turned out to be special hazards for the wolves. Walking through the dense growth of the refuge was difficult, but trotting along a road was easy. Many of the wolves used roads to get around, and two were hit by cars and died. When the batteries on the collars wore out after a few months, the wolves had to be recaptured so that new collars could be put on them. Biologists and citizens alike were relieved when the wolves were successfully captured because it reassured them that if a wolf got into trouble, it could be caught again.

Two females produced litters of pups the first spring, proving that they could thrive in the wild. The young animals grew up and learned how to hunt and avoid danger.

More wolves were released in 1988, and by the end of 1994, 85 percent of the forty-three wolves at Alligator River had been wild born. The red wolf biologists were proud and relieved. They had proven that a predator could be bred for several generations in captivity and still know how to live and reproduce in the wild once again given the chance. The success of the red wolf program was good news for biologists working with other endangered predators. The red wolf biologists expect that more than a hundred wolves will soon be living wild on the refuge.

As more and more red wolves roam eastern North Carolina, the chances of them getting into trouble with people increase. Biologists are finding out that the wolves need rather large territories. Another refuge near Alligator River, called Pocosin Lakes National Wildlife Refuge, also provides good red wolf habitat, but it only has enough room for two additional packs

Biologists keep track of the wolves' locations to help avoid clashes with people.

of wolves. The refuges just aren't big enough for all the wolves, so some have settled on nearby private land. In addition, private land between the two refuges needs to be available to the animals.

Many landowners don't mind sharing their property with wolves, but others are nervous just knowing the animals are there. So far, the red wolf biologists have found ways of dealing with these problems. Private lands are brought into the restoration program through one of several methods. Landowners willing to tolerate wolves may be paid money for their cooperation. Some farmers also welcome the wolves since they can help control populations of pests such as raccoons, nutria, and white-tailed deer. Since 1987, about 250,000 acres of private and state lands have been brought into the program, making it easier for the wolves to roam freely between the two refuges.

The U.S. Fish and Wildlife Service changed the rules in 1995 to allow people more freedom in dealing with potential problems with the wolves. Under the new rules, landowners are allowed to harass the wolves into leaving their land. If the wolves still won't go, the service must remove them. If a

Red wolf pups

Red wolves have proven that they can reproduce in the wild just as easily as they can in captivity. As long as there are enough wildlands for them, they will thrive in their habitats without help from humans.

farmer catches a wolf in the act of killing livestock, he can kill the wolf without penalty, and if a wolf is killed accidentally, there will be no penalty. The red wolf has made such a success of life in the wild that its survival seems assured as long as humans will tolerate its presence. As Gary Henry, coordinator of the Red Wolf Recovery Project, puts it, "Managing the wolves is easy. Managing people is the problem."

Because the wolves at Alligator River have done so well, other sites for wolf reintroduction are desirable. The Great Smoky Mountains National Park and surrounding area is over 1.5 million acres of land belonging to the federal government. This would seem to be plenty of room for a healthy wolf population, but the park may have too many coyotes and not enough prey for the wolves. In 1991, 1992, and 1994, red wolves were released in the park. Besides problems with the wolves interacting with coyotes, nearby residents' distrust of the federal government and/or the wolves has also created some problems. Educational efforts and wolf releases continue, and we can hope that eventually red wolves will again roam freely in these wild places.

The Black-Footed Ferret

FOR YEARS I'D WANTED TO SEE a black-footed ferret, and at last I had the chance to be in a room full of them. But first, I had to make sure I wouldn't bring any germs into their home. In the past, diseases had brought near disaster to the ferrets, and we all wanted to prevent a new epidemic. I stepped into the dressing room at the breeding facility at Sybille, Wyoming, removed my clothes, and entered the shower, where I soaped thoroughly, including washing my hair. The room on the other side of the shower held an assortment of dark blue coveralls, each with a Wyoming Fish and Game Department patch. I found one that fit and struggled into it, then located a pair of thongs for my feet. I was ready to meet the ferrets.

Black-footed ferrets are normally shy, but it was feeding time. As my guide, biologist Tom Thorne, and I passed its cage, each animal rose on its hind legs, nose sniffing the air,

*A rare sight—a black-footed
ferret in the wild*

checking to see if we had the food; we didn't. But the technician who did wasn't far behind us. With an ice-cream scoop, she doled out each animal's ration from a mixture of dark red ground meat and mink chow. As soon as its food appeared, the ferret headed for the pile, grabbed a mouthful, and scurried down its artificial tunnel to the nest box below. After stashing the food, it returned for more until the pile was gone. Then the ferret disappeared to feed in the dark safety of its nest. As the feeding ended, the sound of tiny claws scratching on plywood cage floors gradually subsided until there was silence. Only a few older ferrets remained in sight, not bothering to carry their food to their nests.

Like the red wolf, the black-footed ferret *(Mustela nigripes)* is an endangered species. With its black mask and long, brown-shaded body, this small predator is beautiful and appealing. The black-footed ferret disappeared from the wild because people waged war on the prairie dog, which provided both food and habitat to the ferret. Without prairie dogs to eat and prairie dog burrows to live in, the black-footed ferret was doomed.

Before the European settlement of the American West, prairie dogs lived across the Great Plains, which cover the center of the North American continent. A hundred years ago, there were almost 700 million acres of prairie dog habitat ranging from southern Saskatchewan down into northern Mexico. Prairies covered most of the states of Montana, Wyoming, Colorado, New Mexico, South Dakota, Nebraska, Kansas, and large portions of North Dakota and Oklahoma. Trapping records show that black-footed ferrets occurred over almost the identical range, although none had been recorded from Mexico.

In captivity, each ferret is given its own cage joined by a flexible plastic tube to a den site box below. The tube mimics a prairie dog burrow. Although each animal also has another den site box at cage level, the animals prefer to use the lower den.

A ferret peeks out of the hole in its cage that leads to the nest box.

Millions of prairie dogs once lived across the American plains.

During the late 1800s and early 1900s, the vast majority of prairie habitat became farmland, leaving only 5 to 10 percent of the original prairie dog habitat for the animals. The prairie dogs were also poisoned in huge numbers because they were considered to be pests. What colonies remained were small and scattered. This elimination and fragmentation of its prey's habitat reduced the black-footed ferret to very small numbers. By the 1960s, only ten U.S. counties and Canadian provinces reported having black-footed ferrets. Their numbers continued to fall throughout the 1970s. By 1980, this unique animal appeared headed for extinction.

In 1981, a ferret population was discovered near Meeteetse, Wyoming. The ferrets seemed to be healthy and even increasing in numbers until 1985, when the prairie dogs in the area were hit by a fatal epidemic of sylvatic plague. They died off quickly. As their prey disappeared, ferret numbers decreased rapidly. The final blow was another deadly disease, canine distemper, which hit the ferrets themselves and was discovered in October. The scientists studying the ferrets felt they had no choice but to bring the eighteen survivors into captivity.

Hard work and research paid off. Earlier attempts to breed the ferrets in captivity had failed, but the Wyoming scientists discovered ways to encourage the ferrets to breed and to raise their young successfully. In preparing to raise black-footed ferrets, the biologists experimented with its close relative, the Siberian polecat. By learning how to take care of and breed polecats, they found methods that could work with black-footed ferrets. By 1995, a few hundred black-footed ferrets were living at seven breeding facilities around the country and in Canada.

The ferrets are nervous animals, easy to upset. Researchers have learned to respect and deal with the animals' need for privacy and minimal contact with humans. One of the most important tools in working with the ferrets is a small wire transfer device, like a miniature cage. When a ferret needs to be moved from one place to another, it is coaxed into one of these devices. Human workers can examine the animal, give it necessary shots, or just move it from one place to another with minimal disturbance. The close contact between the ferret's body and the cage feels similar to being in a tunnel. Some of the ferrets get so used to the device that they climb right in when it is put into their cage.

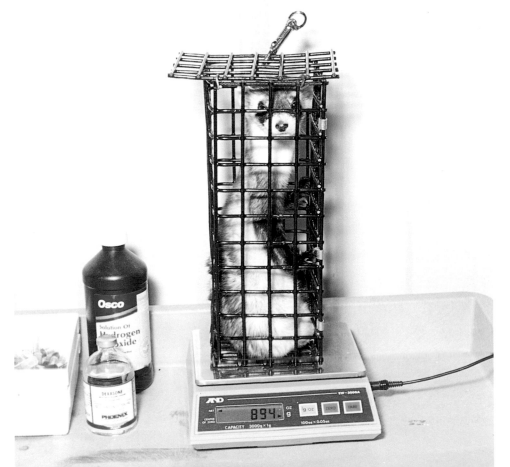

The ferrets are handled as little as possible by humans. When they need to be moved, examined, given immunizations, and weighed, they are carried in this simple metal cage.

Getting secretive animals like ferrets to breed in captivity can be a challenge. Since only a few animals made up the founding stock of all captive ferrets today, matings must be carefully arranged to reduce inbreeding as much as possible. When she is ready to mate, the female is brought to the chosen male's cage for breeding, which takes place at night. Biologists use television monitors to keep track of the ferrets' activities without disturbing them. If the pairing doesn't result in mating, the female is matched with a second male. Sometimes she needs to be paired with three males before mating occurs.

When a pairing works, the female is put with the male for two nights in a row. As the time of birth approaches, the female's cage is cleaned thoroughly and she is left alone. The cages next to hers may not be cleaned for a couple of days in order not to disturb her at this vital time.

Like mating, birth takes place at night. Forty-two days after conception, the female gives birth to from one to eight young. A couple of days later, technicians carefully block the female from the nest box, check the health of the baby ferrets, called kits, and clean the box. They must be very careful since the greatest number of fatalities for ferrets occurs around the time of birth, and every animal is precious.

Unless there is more than one kit, the mother's body doesn't produce enough milk. A single kit must be taken away and put with a different mother. The new mother may either be another ferret or a Siberian polecat, which make better substitute—or surrogate—mothers than the ferrets because they are less nervous around people. Ferret kits are also placed with surrogate mothers if their own mother proves to be negligent. At the facility in Sybille, 20 percent of the kits end up being raised by a foster mother instead of their own.

Raising ferrets in captivity isn't easy. The environment of a wooden nest box in a cage in a room full of ferret cages is very different from the dark, damp peace and quiet of a burrow six to eight feet underground. Even with the best of care, 25 to 40 percent of the kits die before becoming independent of their mothers. One key factor in keeping the youngsters alive, healthy, and growing is the kit care program. When the kits are four weeks of age, a technician blocks the mother away from them twice a day, cleans the nest box thoroughly, and feeds the kits a gruel of ferret food mixed with an artificial milk replacer. The kits are very messy eaters and get the stuff all over their fur. Each animal is sure to be well fed because

Young black-footed ferret kits

it licks food from the coats of its littermates. The liquid in the gruel helps provide the kits with adequate fluid. The air in the room can be quite dry compared to the moisture-saturated air in a burrow, and their small bodies need plenty of fluid to stay healthy.

During the years that the captive breeding program has existed, scientists have studied many aspects of ferret life. One of their most important discoveries is that the food the animals receive from the age of 60 to 120 days becomes their preferred diet throughout their life, so the captive ferrets receive prairie dogs to eat during that time.

The goal of the black-footed ferret recovery plan is to establish at least ten wild populations totaling fifteen hundred breeding animals by the year 2010. At the same time, a breeding population of 240 animals will remain in captivity.

Like the red wolves, ferrets must gain some experience living in a natural habitat and hunting for themselves. Some of the ferrets are placed in outdoor cages with prairie dogs to make sure they know how to capture and kill their prey. When the time comes for their release, the chosen ferrets are locked into their nest boxes and taken to the release site. So far, ferrets have been released in the Shirley Basin of Wyoming, the U. L. Bend National Wildlife Refuge in Montana, and also in Badlands National Park, South Dakota.

Since they will kill ferrets, coyotes are often removed from the release area until the ferrets know their way around and can quickly find the protection of a known burrow if a predator threatens. Even with help from biologists, though, most of the ferrets die before they can learn how to survive and hunt

Black-footed ferrets are being released at the U. L. Bend National Wildlife Refuge in Montana.

successfully on their own, which is also true of wild-born young ferrets. In the summer of 1994, almost all the ferrets in the Shirley Basin disappeared. Two especially violent thunderstorms had swept through the area, flooding burrows and pounding the ground with hailstones. The storms almost certainly killed some of the ferrets. In 1995, prairie dog populations in the Shirley Basin were so low that no ferrets were released there that year. The goal of the Wyoming recovery program is for 20 percent of the ferrets to survive the first

In Montana, ferrets are being reintroduced using a soft-release method. They are brought to the site in their familiar nest boxes, which are placed in the ground. The animals are immediately familiar with the surroundings in their new home.

A black-footed ferret peeks out from a prairie dog burrow.

(M. R. Matchett, U.S. Fish and Wildlife Service)

When a burrow containing a ferret is located, a ring that will pick up the signal from the computer chip in the ferret's neck is placed over the hole. An antenna that can read the signal is nearby.

month and for 10 percent to make it until the next summer. It's encouraging to know that females have already given birth to kits in the wild in all three locations.

In Montana, the ferrets are being followed closely after release. Each ferret has a tiny computer chip under the skin on its head. Each chip identifies the animal individually. Every week, biologists head for the refuge to check on the ferrets. Since ferrets are nocturnal animals, night is also the time for ferret watching. Bright lights catch the unique shine of the ferrets' eyes, and during the winter, tracks on the snow show which burrows the ferrets use. When a ferret is spotted in a particular burrow, the biologists put a special metal ring around the burrow opening, and they lay a signal-reading device on the ground. When the ferret pops its head up again, the ring picks up the signal from the computer chip under the skin and indicates the identity of the individual. The exact location of each ferret is pinpointed by way of satellite. By keeping close track of the location and numbers of the ferrets, the Montana researchers can get an idea of what encourages both the death and the survival of newly wild black-footed ferrets. The knowledge they gain with time and patience can help bring increasing success to the ferret reintroduction program.

The Golden Lion Tamarin

WHEN I FIRST SAW A GOLDEN LION TAMARIN, I was amazed at its size. I had seen this beautiful monkey gracing the covers of wildlife magazines, filling the entire page with its flaming orange, intelligent face. But the real thing was a tiny fellow— just as brilliantly colored but weighing only a little more than a pound—smaller than the tiniest adult dog. His miniature hands enchanted me, their slender fingers ending in sharp clawlike nails, his little feet the same. The size and delicacy of the animal seemed to reflect its precarious situation in the world. The home of the tamarin has become the part of Brazil most densely populated by people. Between 90 and 98 percent of its rain forest habitat has been destroyed, and remnants of the population have been taken into captivity for breeding so the tamarin can be returned to the wild.

The golden lion tamarin *(Leontopithecus rosalia rosalia)* lives in small family groups up in the branches of the rain forest

The golden lion tamarin

trees. They sleep at night in their tree hole nest or in dense vine tangles and search for food—fruit, insects, lizards, birds, and other small animals—by day. The female usually gives birth to one set of twins each year. Both parents as well as older brothers and sisters help take care of the babies. The family travels through the trees together, with the older animals carrying the youngsters. When the young females are ready to mate, between eighteen and twenty-four months old, the mother chases them away. They find their own mates and start new families. The young males stay with their biological families longer, but they also soon leave to pursue families of their own.

Some of the tamarin's native rain forest home in Brazil has been protected as part of a biological reserve. The conservation plan calls for reforesting some of the areas where trees have been cut down to connect isolated patches of rain forest and allow the tamarins to make contact with one another. By the year 2025, biologists hope that two thousand tamarins will roam through an area four times as large as the present protected forests.

Conservation groups in Brazil are helping to make this goal possible by educating people about the importance of preserving animals like the tamarin. Some ranchers now welcome this forest monkey onto their property and take great pride in their resident tamarins. The reserve and ranches provide an opportunity for some of the tamarins born in zoos to return to their natural homes.

Helping tamarins learn about life in the wild is difficult in a zoo environment. Zoo animals quickly learn the confines of

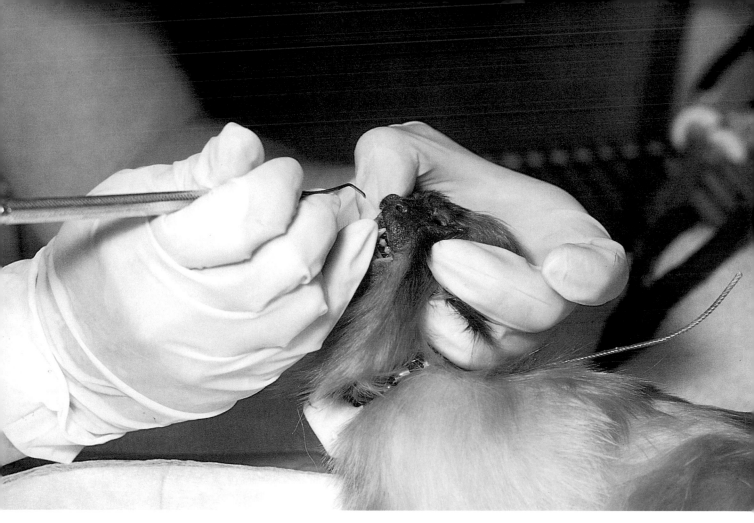

Zookeepers take very good care of these valuable animals. Here, one is getting its teeth cleaned.

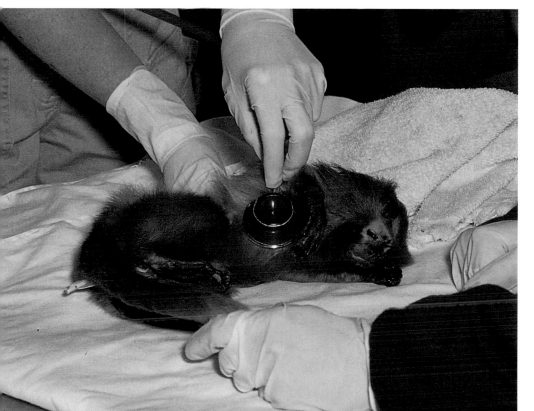

Its heart rate and respiration are also checked.

their restricted enclosures. Any trees or poles for climbing are usually stout and sturdy, and the animals never have to search for their food. It is brought to them on a regular schedule, so the animals learn when and where to expect it. Everything presented to them as food is safe to eat, and they are never threatened by predators.

Wild tamarins, however, live in a completely different world. Traveling involves leaping from tree to tree, often on swaying vines or slender branches. Food in the rain forest is scattered, and the monkeys must search for it. They must know what foods are safe to eat and what might be deadly, and they must be on the lookout for predators such as poisonous snakes.

In order to prepare tamarins for release into the wild, biologists must create a zoo environment that comes closer to their natural habitat. Their nest box is anchored in a tree on the zoo grounds instead of in a cage, and the monkeys are free

The tamarins are very attached to their nest boxes. One is shown here in the exhibit area of the zoo.

The caretakers keep away from the tamarins as much as possible. Food is hauled up to the tamarins on a pulley.

to explore. Because they are very attached to their nest box, the tamarins do not leave the zoo. Swaying ropes, which imitate forest vines, are strung in the trees around the nest box, and the animals are fed on an irregular schedule. Sometimes food is hidden away from the nest box so the monkeys must search to find it.

The monkeys' tails are dyed with individual patterns for identification, and they are fitted with radio collars. That way,

When the monkeys are released onto the zoo grounds,
their nest box goes with them so they stay close to home.

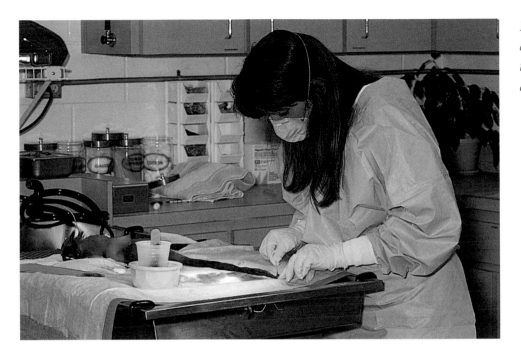

*Before being released
onto the zoo grounds,
the tamarins' tails are
dyed for identification.*

scientists can identify each monkey by sight and also by the signal its collar sends.

When it is time to release a group of tamarins into the wild, the animals are flown to Brazil. Along the way, the monkeys are taken care of, receiving plenty of food and water. An entire family may be released together, or a single animal might be paired with a previously reintroduced individual.

Many things in the rain forest are different from the familiar environment of a zoo, so the animals do best if introduced to their new homes gradually. At first, nest boxes are set in cages in the forest. The tamarins can learn to eat insects and small lizards that enter the cage, and they can get accustomed to the steamy tropical heat. Their ears become used to the forest sounds.

After some time in the cage, the monkeys are closed up in their nest box, and the box is hoisted up and anchored in a

This pair of tamarins is free to explore the zoo grounds.

forest tree—the tamarins' new home. A feeding platform is added so the monkeys can be fed while they get used to taking care of themselves.

At least one animal in each group wears a radio collar, and each individual can be identified by its tail pattern and another distinctive mark on its body. Human observers take careful notes on the animals' behavior, watching to see when and how they learn to find and capture food on their own. Bit by bit over the weeks ahead, the food is moved farther away from the nest box, and it is provided less and less frequently.

Even with such careful treatment, only about 30 percent of captive-born tamarins released into the wild survive longer than two years. Some die from eating poisonous plants; others are eaten by predators. But the ones that survive and go on to reproduce in the wild give hope for the future. Their offspring grow up wild in their natural home, learning the survival skills necessary for living in the hazardous rain forest. The most recent reports indicate that 25 of the 141 reintroduced tamarins survived. These animals had given birth to 175 young, 100 of which were still alive—making a total of 125 individuals living in the wild as a result of the reintroduction program.

CHAPTER 5

Leaping Lemurs

FOR MONTHS, Bill Muñoz had been telling me about the wonderful facilities for lemurs at the Duke University Primate Center in North Carolina, so I was more than ready for our visit. To get to the lemurs, our host, David Haring, led us through the trees to a gate in a very tall fence. Plastic tags clipped to the fencing indicated which individual animals lived here. We entered and closed the gate behind us. I felt as if I was on a wildlife expedition in a faraway place. The woods within the fencing were quite dense, and we had to pick our way through them to reach the cage in which the lemurs spend the night. David opened the cage door, and within seconds, the lemurs climbed out, then leaped gracefully from tree trunk to tree trunk like giant furry frogs, staring at us with their intense gaze. These were sifakas—rare leaf eaters seldom found in captivity. I was enthralled. We continued to watch as the

Sifakas are striking-looking lemurs.

Brown lemurs

lemurs performed their morning explorations, climbing a tree here, nibbling a leaf there. They were completely at home in the North Carolina woods.

All lemur species are endangered residents of the large tropical island of Madagascar, off the eastern coast of Africa. Madagascar is home to thousands of unique and endangered species of both plants and animals. Most of the island's lush forests have been cut down. Other habitats have been destroyed as well, and many of the threatened species are hunted for food. Lemurs are probably the best known of Madagascar's endangered wildlife. They are primates, like tamarins and orangutans, but they are considered to be more "primitive," closer to the original ancestors that eventually evolved into the many different types of primates.

Even though they are endangered, at least a few lemurs of each species still cling to survival in the wild. Because so little natural lemur habitat is left, individuals of many species have

The ring-tailed lemur is a popular animal in many zoos.

been taken into captivity and scientists have worked toward breeding them, not always an easy task. Some still won't breed in captivity, but ways have been found for others. The mongoose lemur, for example, would breed when first brought in from the wild, then stopped. Duke researchers have found that the female mongoose lemurs got too fat eating the rich food given them in captivity. After receiving a leaner diet, they lost weight and began reproducing again in the early 1990s. Because of its success with the mongoose lemurs, Duke has been sending them to other institutions where breeding pairs now live. Sifakas once refused to reproduce in captivity, too, until Duke scientists found that the animals would breed if kept in natural light and were fed natural vegetation rather than dried food.

Because natural conditions were so beneficial to the animals, the researchers decided to build large outdoor enclosures to provide as normal a life as possible to the captives. It would be years before lemurs could go home to the forests of Madagascar, and living out-of-doors in the meantime would give them a better chance of survival once it was possible to reintroduce them. While both people and animals waited, scientists could study the lemurs' behavior to learn as much about them as possible.

When Duke scientists first proposed releasing lemurs into the enclosures, some people predicted disaster. One concern was that the animals would eat plants that were toxic to them and die. But feeding trials showed that the lemurs were very selective about which leaves to eat—they sniffed and nibbled first, rejecting poisonous ones. Some scientists still had worries. They feared that the lemurs would behave like cage-reared apes and just sit on the ground, waiting to be fed. And scientists thought that if they did try to climb, they would misjudge leaping distances and fall, or would be captured by predators like

Lemurs like this crowned sifaka quickly learn which leaves and fruits in the North Carolina woods are safe to eat.

owls or hawks. Fortunately, these worries proved to be largely unfounded. The lemurs took to the woods easily, foraging carefully on safe leaves, learning quickly how to move through the forest, and avoiding predators quite effectively. A few young ring-tailed lemurs were taken by a predator, and some animals have been injured in falls, but such losses have been minimal.

Three species of lemurs lived in the enclosure we first entered—sifakas *(Propithecus verreauxi coquereli)*, brown lemurs *(Eulemur fulvus)*, and ruffed lemurs *(Varecia variegata)*. The lemurs at Duke are in especially good health. The enclosures are large enough to give them room to roam, keeping their bodies fit, and some of the plants provide natural food, so the lemurs learn to forage for themselves as well as to eat what their keepers provide for them. They also have the opportunity to interact freely with other animals—not only their own kind but other species of lemur as well. When animals from Duke are chosen for release into the wild, they will be well prepared.

The Duke Primate Center is heavily involved in conservation efforts in Madagascar. Duke scientists conduct studies involving the populations and ecology of endangered lemurs. Staff members provide advice for developing parks and preserves in Madagascar, and they help educate forest reserve workers and the public. If lemurs are ever to be successfully reintroduced, they will need well-protected forests and a public that welcomes their return.

Much of the research conducted at Duke focuses on problems related to reintroduction. Although the familiar ring-tailed lemur is endangered in the wild, it thrives in zoos around the world. At Duke, techniques may first be tested on ring-tailed lemurs before being used on other, more rare and delicate species.

The first reintroduction effort using lemurs at Duke will involve the black-and-white ruffed lemur *(Varecia variegata variegata),* a striking animal that has done well at Duke and other institutions. The Betampona reserve in Madagascar is one of the few remaining examples of eastern lowland forest in the country. It is small, but a number of lemur species live

there, including a few black-and-white ruffed lemurs. The reserve's small size and isolation from other forests result in both advantages and disadvantages for reintroduced animals. A small preserve is easier to protect and monitor. If introducing animals brings a negative effect, such as disease, any damage will be limited to a small area. Isolation, though, also means that limited populations cannot interbreed with other groups.

At least eighteen months before release the lemurs will be sent to Madagascar, where they will be kept in enclosures. This is necessary because the island is in the Southern Hemisphere,

The male black lemur has blue eyes.

Ruffed lemurs will be the first kind released into the wild in the Duke program. The lessons learned from these releases will make future reintroductions of more seriously endangered lemurs much smoother.

and the lemurs' reproductive cycles have to adjust to the different seasonal cycle below the equator. A few animals are already in Madagascar awaiting release.

The reintroduced animals' behavior and health will be carefully monitored. By studying the successes and failures of this program, scientists will be better able to plan releases back to the wild of other, more highly endangered lemurs in the future.

The female black lemur isn't black at all, and her eyes are brown,

Hope and Disappointment

As we've seen, attempts to reintroduce mammals into their former homes have met with both success and disappointment. As of 1993, reintroductions of 126 different animal species, from fish to foxes, had been attempted. Sixteen of the projects had succeeded to the point of creating a self-sustaining wild population. That means at least five hundred animals of each kind living wild and free.

Most species of rhinoceros are endangered, and reintroductions of animals bred in zoos have been made. Rhino populations must be carefully guarded, though, to prevent poaching. The rhinoceros's horn has many uses in native medicines and is worth more than gold to some cultures. In areas where these cultures exist, authorities have actually sawed off the horns of some of the animals in an attempt to protect them from being killed.

Rhinoceroses, like this black rhino, were once common in parts of Africa and Asia. Now, they are endangered wherever they live. But reintroducing them into the wild must wait until safe places exist for these valuable animals.

The reintroduction of the Arabian oryx *(Oryx leucoryx)* has been a continuing success story. This beautiful animal with long, slender horns has been reintroduced into much of its former desert habitat. The last known wild oryx were killed in 1972, but luckily, a number of Arab countries had established captive herds in the 1950s. Some were also sent to the United States and became the nucleus of a captive breeding program.

During the 1980s, these Arabian oryx were returned to Oman and Jordan, and captive breeding efforts began in Saudi Arabia in 1986. In 1990, oryx were released in one reserve in Saudi Arabia. The release was so successful that the population

Right: The Przewalski's horse is the last remaining species of wild horse.

has become self-sustaining. In 1995, oryx and another endangered species called the sand gazelle were released into a different protected area where the species had not been seen for over thirty years.

Reintroduction efforts often run into unexpected problems. The only surviving species of true wild horse *(Equus przewalskii)* became extinct in the wild in 1968. Fortunately, the Przewalski's horse breeds well in captivity and the species was able to sustain itself. As a matter of fact, many of the horses in zoos today are not allowed to breed as there is no place to put them in zoos or the wild.

Governments and conservation organizations want this hardy horse to return to its previous homes in Mongolia, China, and the former Soviet Union. But finding a good reintroduction

site where these horses once roamed is turning out to be difficult. A herd was established in Mongolia, only fifty-six miles (ninety kilometers) from the capital city of Ulan Bator. This area is used by many people, so herdsmen must keep the Przewalski's horses from leaving the reserve and wandering into conflict with humans. The animals are doing well, but research has shown that this region wasn't originally home to the Przewalski's horses after all. Since the goal of reintroduction is to return species to their original homes, other sites need to be found where the horses did once live and where they don't have to be tended. One area of the Gobi desert, the last known wild home of this species, is a strong possibility, but human use of the area for livestock grazing needs to be controlled before the horse can truly live wild again.

The Florida panther is not a unique species in itself, but a variety, or subspecies, of the cougar *(Felis concolor)*. Only about fifty of these panthers live in the wild, and biologists are hoping that captive-bred individuals can be set free. But because so few animals remain, inbreeding has become a problem. Genetic studies have shown that the Florida panthers living wild today are actually quite different from the original animals. Pet cougars from Central America were released in Florida, and these animals interbred with the panthers. Since the wild panthers are not pure Florida panthers, biologists have decided to introduce the closest wild relative, the Texas cougar, into Florida to boost populations and to reduce inbreeding of the few remaining animals. Reintroduction of captive-bred animals probably won't be enough to save the original Florida panther.

The Florida panther's numbers and its habitat have become so reduced that many people believe it cannot be saved.

The Florida panther is a subspecies of the cougar, or mountain lion, shown here as a cub.

This Florida panther cub looks very much like its close relative, the mountain lion.

Captive breeding is a very expensive proposition. Not everyone believes the money is well spent. The golden lion tamarin project, which is seen as an especially successful program, averages a cost of $22,000 for each surviving monkey. The lion-tailed macaque is a highly endangered monkey that lives in India. An Indian biologist has calculated that reintroducing a dozen macaques into their natural habitat would cost $150,000 but that only $30,000 each year would pay the salary for enough guards to protect the habitat for 250 to 300 monkeys.

Keeping animals that are not involved in reintroduction programs in zoos is expensive as well. Maintaining healthy captive populations of five monkey species in a zoo costs about a half million dollars a year. That amount of money would pay the total costs for maintaining the entire Serengeti National Park in Tanzania, including guards and upkeep. But without zoo populations, hundreds of species of vertebrate animals, from fish to apes, would quickly disappear from the planet, never to be seen again. Both wild habitats and zoos are important to maintaining the diversity of life. Zoos have the added benefit of giving people the opportunity to see and learn about wild animals from around the earth.

The best answer to protecting wild animals and plants is to preserve their habitats in the first place. Whenever a forest is cut for timber or a grassland is plowed under to create farmland, the homes of wild things disappear. Fortunately, zoos around the world are beginning to support research on wild populations of animals, and they help pay the expenses of parks and preserves where animals still live wild. Not only is habitat preservation cheaper than reintroduction, it is much less risky and better for the animals themselves. But as long as animals living wild are endangered, captive breeding with an eye to reintroduction is an important and hopeful tool for the conservation of a number of species around the world.

INDEX

A

Alligator River National Wildlife Refuge, North Carolina, 18, 19, 25
American Zoo Association, 10

B

Badlands National Park, South Dakota, 36
Betampona reserve, 56–57
birds, 10
bison, 5–7, 8
Brazil, 40, 42

C

cougar, Texas, 64
coyotes, 36

D

Duke University Primate Center, North Carolina, 50, 53–56

E

endangered species, breeding, 9–10
Endangered Species Act, 15, 18

F

ferret, black-footed, 28–39
    kits, 34–36
    mating, 34
    recovery plan, 36

G

Great Smoky Mountains National Park, 27

H

habitat, loss of, 4
Haring, David, 50
Henry, Gary, 27
horse, Przewalski's, 63–64

I

IUCN, 10

L

lemurs, 50–59. *See also* sifakas
    black, 58, 59
    brown, 52, 55
    mongoose, 53
    ring-tailed, 53, 55, 56
    ruffed, 55, 57, 58

M

macaque, lion-tailed, 66
Madagascar, 52, 54, 56–59
Mongolia, 64
monkeys, 66–67

O

orangutan, 7–9
oryx, Arabian, 62–63

P

panther, Florida, 64–66
Pocosin Lakes National
    Wildlife Refuge,
    North Carolina, 25–26
polecat, Siberian, 32–33
prairie dogs, 30–32
predators, 9. *See also* specific species

R

rain forest, destruction of, 2–4
Red Data Book, 10
rhinoceroses, 60–61

S

serval, 6
Shirley Basin, Wyoming, 36–37
sifakas, 51
    crowned, 54
Smith, Roland, 12
Species Survival Plan, 10–11

T

tamarin, golden lion, 40–49
    survival rate in wild, 49

Thorne, Tom, 28

U

U. L. Bend National Wildlife
    Refuge, Montana, 36, 39

W

wisent, 7
wolf
    gray, 14
    Mexican gray, 11
    Recovery Plan, 15
    red, 12–27

Z

zoo ark, 5
zoos, 4–5, 42–47, 66–67